D1397755

TODAY'S 12 HOTTEST
NFL SUPERSTARS

by Tom Robinson

www.12StoryLibrary.com

12-Story Library is an imprint of Peterson Publishing Company and Press Room Editions.

Produced for 12-Story Library by Red Line Editorial

Photographs ©: Jim Mahoney/AP Images, cover, 1; Tom DiPace/AP Images, 4; G. Newman Lowrance/AP Images, 5, 20; Action Sports Photography/Shutterstock Images, 6; Patrick Semansky/AP Images, 7, 18; Charlie Riedel/AP Images, 8, 28; Paul Spinelli/AP Images, 9, 11; Ed Rieker/AP Images, 10; Marcio Jose Sanchez/AP Images, 12; Evan Pinkus/AP Images, 13; Damian Strohmeyer/AP Images, 14; Frank Franklin II/AP Images, 15; Nick Wass/AP Images, 16, 29; Kevin Terrell/AP Images, 19; Greg Trott/AP Images, 22; Morry Gash/AP Images, 23; Ted S. Warren/AP Images, 24; Tom Hauck/AP Images, 25; Aaron M. Sprecher/AP Images, 26; John Raoux/AP Images, 27

ISBN
978-1-63235-022-0 (hardcover)
978-1-63235-082-4 (paperback)
978-1-62143-063-6 (hosted ebook)

Library of Congress Control Number: 2014946801

Printed in the United States of America
Mankato, MN
October, 2014

Go beyond the book. Get free, up-to-date content on this topic at 12StoryLibrary.com.

TABLE OF CONTENTS

TOM BRADY LEADS NEW ENGLAND PATRIOTS TO FIVE SUPER BOWLS

Tom Brady did not play football until ninth grade. That put him behind other players his age. Still, he became a standout high school quarterback. He played college football for the University of Michigan. Other quarterbacks on the team were more heavily recruited. Brady sat on the bench for two seasons. But when he got on the field, Brady was there to stay. He set many school records. He became one of the best quarterbacks in the game.

New England picked Brady in the sixth round of the NFL Draft in 2000. Many sixth-round picks

Brady helped beat the St. Louis Rams in the Super Bowl after the 2001 season.

never make it. Brady was different. When starting quarterback Drew Bledsoe got hurt, Brady showed he was ready to fill his shoes. Brady played so well that he took over permanently. In his second year as a pro, he led the Patriots to the Super Bowl. Fame followed after Brady helped New England win against the St. Louis Rams. Brady led the Patriots to five Super Bowls through the 2013 season. The Patriots won three of them. Many people call him the best quarterback of all time.

27

The age by which Brady had started and won three Super Bowls.

Birth Date: August 3, 1977
Birthplace: San Mateo, California
Height: 6 feet 4 (1.93 m)
Weight: 225 pounds (102 kg)
Team: New England Patriots, 2000–
Breakthrough Season: Took over as starting quarterback in 2001 and led Patriots to Super Bowl title
Awards: Super Bowl Most Valuable Player (MVP) after 2001 and 2003 seasons, NFL MVP 2007 and 2010, first-team quarterback on Pro Football Hall of Fame all-2000s team

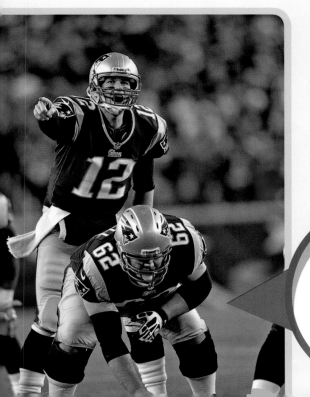

Brady calls out signals just before the snap during a 2013 game against the Baltimore Ravens.

DREW BREES BECOMES SUPER BOWL MVP

Drew Brees came to the New Orleans Saints from the San Diego Chargers in 2006. He was trying to rebuild his career after a shoulder injury. New Orleans was also recovering. The city was hit hard by Hurricane Katrina in 2005.

Brees and the Saints rebuilt together. Brees became known for his involvement in the community. He thrived on the field, too. Brees was named Super Bowl MVP in 2010, after leading the Saints past the Indianapolis Colts.

Brees led the New Orleans Saints to their first Super Bowl.

BREES DREAM FOUNDATION

Brees and his wife, Brittany, started the Brees Dream Foundation in 2003. The foundation has donated almost $20 million to charities. The donations help cancer patients and families in need. In 2006, Brees received the NFL Walter Payton Man of the Year award. The award recognizes charity work and on-field excellence.

Brees is small for an NFL quarterback. But he succeeds with a strong and accurate arm. Brees has proved his lack of size is not a problem. He was picked for the Pro Bowl every year from 2008 to 2013.

2006

Year Brees received the NFL Walter Payton Man of the Year award.

Birth Date: January 15, 1979

Birthplace: Austin, Texas

Height: 6 feet (1.83 m)

Weight: 209 pounds (95 kg)

Teams: San Diego Chargers, 2001–2005; New Orleans Saints, 2006–

Breakthrough Season: Led the NFL in passing yards in 2006

Awards: Super Bowl MVP after 2009 season, NFL Offensive Player of the Year in 2008 and 2011, *Sports Illustrated*'s 2010 Sportsman of the Year

Brees and his wife, Brittany, thank a crowd for donating to the Brees Dream Foundation at a concert in 2009.

JAMAAL CHARLES PROVES A THREAT ON THE FIELD

Jamaal Charles has speed that once made him a track and field star. He earned the bronze medal in the 400-meter hurdles at the 2003 World Youth Championships in Athletics. Charles was also a football star while growing up in Texas. He went on to play college football at the University of Texas. The Kansas City Chiefs drafted him after his third year of college. He was ready to show off his speed on NFL fields.

Even when playing on struggling teams in Kansas City, Charles produced. He could not be stopped. Not even a major knee injury stopped him. Charles had knee surgery in 2011. He came back with his best season in 2012.

Charles uses his speed to run the ball in a 2013 game against the San Diego Chargers.

70

Number of passes Charles caught in 2013.

Birth Date: December 27, 1986

Birthplace: Port Arthur, Texas

Height: 6 feet 1 (1.85 m)

Weight: 200 pounds (91 kg)

Team: Kansas City Chiefs, 2008–

Breakthrough Season: Came back from ACL surgery to rush for 1,509 yards in 2012

Awards: First-team NFL All-Pro 2010 and 2013

the Oakland Raiders. Four of them were on pass receptions. Defenses always have to know where he is, even on pass plays. They have learned that Charles is a threat no matter where he is on the field.

Before his injury, Charles had run for more than 1,000 yards in a season twice. He topped the 1,000-yard mark in each of the first two seasons after his surgery.

The Chiefs built much of their offense around Charles. They found new ways to get him the ball. Charles got better at catching passes. He scored five touchdowns in a game against

Charles finds ways to catch difficult passes.

9

CALVIN JOHNSON BECOMES NFL'S "MEGATRON"

Calvin Johnson's combination of size, strength, and speed has made him a star at every level. He was a football and baseball star at Sandy Creek High School in Georgia. He became a football All-American in college at Georgia Tech. Johnson's fame was made clear in 2012. He was picked for the cover of the video game *Madden NFL 13*. The cover was decided by fan voting. It's not often a wide receiver wins a popularity contest.

Known almost as well by his nickname, "Megatron," Johnson has gained respect from many. He has set many records for his position. Among those was signing the largest contract ever by a receiver. One time in 2011, he caught the ball in the end zone over three Dallas Cowboys. The fourth-quarter touchdown earned a victory for the Lions.

Johnson stands with an enlarged cover of *Madden NFL 13*, featuring himself, in 2012.

1,964

Number of Johnson's receiving yards in 2012 season.

Birth Date: September 29, 1985

Birthplace: Newnan, Georgia

Height: 6 feet 5 (1.96 m)

Weight: 239 pounds (108 kg)

Team: Detroit Lions, 2007–

Breakthrough Season: Set NFL record for most yards receiving in a season in 2012 with 1,964 yards

Awards: First-team NFL All-Pro 2011–13

"MEGATRON"

Detroit Lions teammate Roy Williams gave Johnson the nickname "Megatron" in his rookie year. "Megatron" is a character in the movie *Transformers*. The character is known for his amazing abilities. Johnson has more skills than most wide receivers. He was tested before being picked second overall in the 2007 NFL Draft. The tests showed Johnson was bigger, faster, and could jump higher than other receivers.

Johnson goes over and around defenders to make catches.

LUKE KUECHLY: A TACKLING MACHINE

In high school, Luke Kuechly—pronounced "KEEK-li"—led his football team to a state title. He moved from outside linebacker to middle linebacker early in both his college and pro careers. Kuechly quickly showed he could make the plays the position demands. He often makes more tackles than anyone else in the game.

At Boston College, Kuechly led the NCAA in tackles twice. He led the entire NFL in tackles as a Carolina Panthers rookie in 2012.

Kuechly lines up at middle linebacker. He is the focus of the defense. Kuechly stands

Kuechly (left) sacks San Francisco 49ers quarterback Colin Kaepernick during the fourth quarter of a 2013 game.

behind the linemen and in front of the defensive backs. For decades, middle linebacker was the glamour position for NFL defenses. Modern football has shifted attention to those who rush quarterbacks and cover receivers. Carolina is different. Kuechly is the clear leader of one of the NFL's toughest defenses.

Kuechly was the NFL's top rookie defender in his first year. In 2013, his strong play helped the Panthers get back to the playoffs for the first time in five years.

24

Number of tackles Kuechly recorded in one game, tying the NFL record.

Birth Date: April 20, 1991
Birthplace: Cincinnati, Ohio
Height: 6 feet 3 (1.91 m)
Weight: 242 pounds (110 kg)
Team: Carolina Panthers, 2012–
Breakthrough Season: Started all 16 games as a rookie in 2012
Awards: 2012 NFL Defensive Rookie of the Year, 2013 NFL Defensive Player of the Year

Kuechly was named NFL Defensive Player of the Year in his second season with the Panthers.

6

PEYTON MANNING CLAIMS MULTIPLE NFL MVPS

Peyton Manning gets his job done in many ways. He uses his mind and his mouth before the play starts. After the snap, the quarterback uses his footwork and accurate arm to beat the defense. Quarterbacks are expected to take charge. None in this generation have done that better than Manning.

Manning missed the whole 2011 season with Indianapolis because of neck surgery. When he came back to the game, he signed with the Denver Broncos. In 2013, Manning had the best season of his career. He threw for more yards and touchdowns in one season than any quarterback in NFL history.

Manning went into 2014 ranked second in NFL history in most passing categories. Manning's skills form a rare combination. They have helped make him the NFL MVP five times. No other player has matched that.

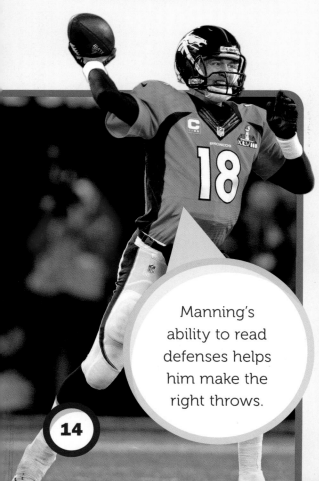

Manning's ability to read defenses helps him make the right throws.

Peyton (left) walks off the field with his brother, Eli (right), after a game in 2013.

5

Number of times Manning has won the NFL MVP award.

Birth Date: March 24, 1976

Birthplace: New Orleans, Louisiana

Height: 6 feet 5 (1.96 m)

Weight: 230 pounds (104 kg)

Teams: Indianapolis Colts, 1998–2011; Denver Broncos, 2012–

Breakthrough Season: Led the NFL in passing yards and won his first MVP award in 2003

Awards: NFL MVP in 2003, 2004, 2008, 2009, and 2013, Super Bowl MVP after 2006 season, 2005 Walter Payton NFL Man of the Year, 2000s *Sports Illustrated's* NFL Player of the Decade, 2013 *Sports Illustrated's* Sportsman of the Year

FAMILY COMPETITION

Manning is not the only NFL quarterback in his family. Archie Manning, Peyton's father, was also a quarterback. He played from 1971 to 1984, mostly with the New Orleans Saints. Eli, Peyton's younger brother, won two Super Bowls with the New York Giants through 2013.

15

LeSEAN McCOY RUNS PHILADELPHIA'S OFFENSE

Blazing speed helped make LeSean McCoy a major prospect as a young player. *ESPN RISE* named him the best sophomore player in the country while at Bishop McDevitt High School in Harrisburg, Pennsylvania. McCoy was then named Player of the Year as a junior. Two outstanding seasons at the University of Pittsburgh made McCoy ready for the NFL.

McCoy leaps over Washington Redskins cornerback E.J. Biggers to score a touchdown in 2013.

McCoy has already become a unique weapon among NFL running backs. Through the years, the league has relied more on specialists. Offenses were once built around a dominant running back. That idea has changed. Today, most teams use running backs less. They split up the duties of the position. But not the Philadelphia Eagles. "Shady" McCoy still does it all. There is no stepping aside on third down for a pass-catching specialist. The Philadelphia Eagles do not turn elsewhere in short-yardage situations. McCoy is an every-down back.

McCoy moves around to different positions in the backfield as needed. He catches passes. He blocks for the quarterback. And, of course, he carries the ball on running plays. The Eagles can rely on him to get the tough yards. McCoy can run around the end or up the middle. His running ability helps set up the rest

1,607
Number of yards McCoy rushed for in 2013.

Birth Date: July 12, 1988
Birthplace: Harrisburg, Pennsylvania
Height: 5 feet 10 (1.78 m)
Weight: 215 pounds (98 kg)
Team: Philadelphia Eagles, 2009–
Breakthrough Season: Became a first-team All-Pro for the first time in 2011
Award: 2013 NFC Offensive Player of the Year

of the Philadelphia offense. McCoy has committed his offseason time to building strength. It has made him a durable NFL running back. He led the NFL in rushing yards in 2013.

PATRICK PETERSON IS A DUAL THREAT

Patrick Peterson is an All-Pro cornerback and punt returner for the Arizona Cardinals. He has been shutting down opposing receivers since his high school days. In 2007, he was named national high school Defensive Player of the Year.

Peterson continued to shine in college at Louisiana State University. He was again considered the top college defensive player in the country in 2010. At the same time, he ranked fourth in the nation by averaging 16.1

Peterson breaks away to return a punt and score a touchdown against the Baltimore Ravens in 2011.

yards per punt return. As an NFL rookie for the Cardinals, Peterson started every game as cornerback. He also became the only player in league history to return four punts for touchdowns of more than 80 yards in the same season.

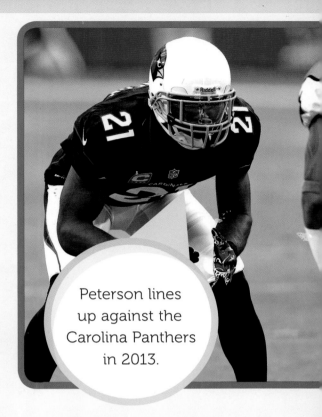

Peterson lines up against the Carolina Panthers in 2013.

4

Number of punt-return touchdowns Peterson scored in 2011, tying an NFL record.

Birth Date: July 11, 1990
Birthplace: Fort Lauderdale, Florida
Height: 6 feet (1.83 m)
Weight: 220 pounds (100 kg)
Team: Arizona Cardinals, 2011–
Breakthrough Season: Became a full-time starter on defense and special teams in his rookie year of 2011
Awards: Pro Bowl, 2011, 2012 and 2013; First-team All-Pro, 2011 and 2013

Peterson's records include the longest punt return in overtime in NFL history. He brought a punt back 99 yards to lift the Cardinals to victory over the St. Louis Rams in 2011.

Peterson was named to the Pro Bowl following each of his first three NFL seasons. He was named All-Pro as a kick returner in 2011. Peterson was honored again in 2013, this time as one of the best two cornerbacks in the NFL.

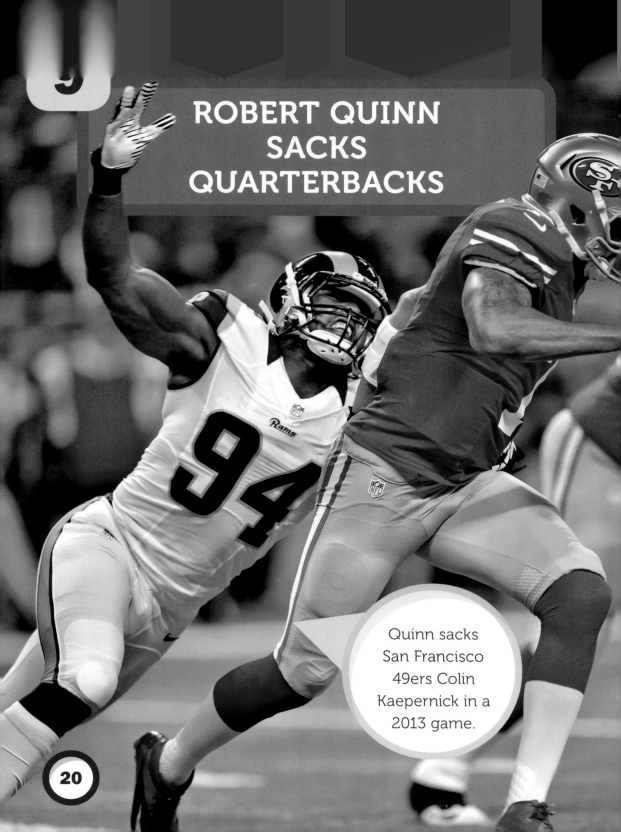

ROBERT QUINN
SACKS
QUARTERBACKS

Quinn sacks San Francisco 49ers Colin Kaepernick in a 2013 game.

Robert Quinn didn't have an easy path to stardom in the NFL. While still in high school, he found out he had a brain tumor. He needed surgery to make it smaller. His senior football season was cut short. But just two months after the surgery, he was ready to compete in sports again.

Quinn recovered in time to win his second South Carolina state wrestling title. The next fall, he was back on the football field for the first of his two seasons at the University of North Carolina. In 2011, the St. Louis Rams selected him in the first round of the draft. He was the fourteenth pick overall.

Quinn was an effective pass rusher as a rookie reserve. His combination of speed and strength turned him into an impact player in 2012. He started 14 games that season and reached double digits in sacks for the first time. By 2013, he was a major force. Quinn set a team record and led the NFC in sacks that

19
Number of sacks Quinn had in 2013.

Birth Date: May 18, 1990
Birthplace: Ladson, South Carolina
Height: 6 feet 4 (1.93 m)
Weight: 270 pounds (122 kg)
Team: St. Louis Rams, 2011–
Breakthrough Season: Led the NFC in sacks and was named to his first Pro Bowl in 2013
Awards: Professional Football Writers of America Defensive Player of the Year, 2013

year with 19. He also was named first-team All-Pro. That meant he was considered the best player in the entire league at his position. The Professional Football Writers of America selected Quinn as the NFL Defensive Player of the Year.

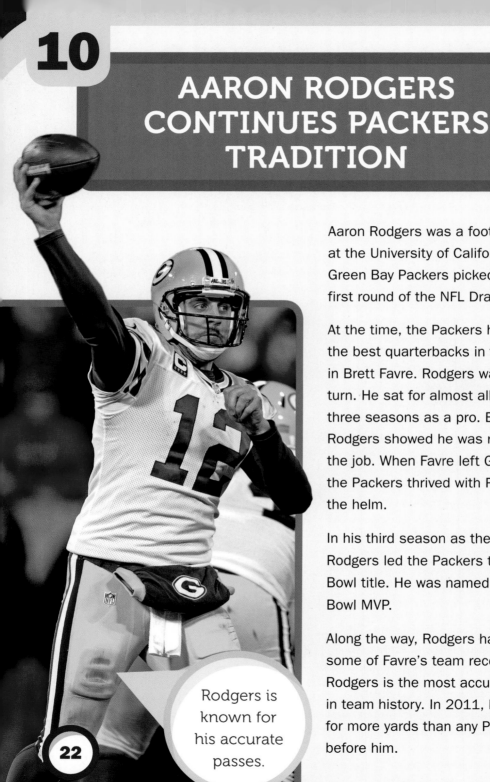

AARON RODGERS CONTINUES PACKERS TRADITION

Aaron Rodgers was a football star at the University of California. The Green Bay Packers picked him in the first round of the NFL Draft in 2005.

At the time, the Packers had one of the best quarterbacks in the NFL in Brett Favre. Rodgers waited his turn. He sat for almost all of his first three seasons as a pro. But then Rodgers showed he was ready for the job. When Favre left Green Bay, the Packers thrived with Rogers at the helm.

In his third season as the starter, Rodgers led the Packers to a Super Bowl title. He was named the Super Bowl MVP.

Along the way, Rodgers has broken some of Favre's team records. Rodgers is the most accurate passer in team history. In 2011, he passed for more yards than any Packer before him.

Rodgers is known for his accurate passes.

Rodgers holds his Super Bowl MVP trophy in 2011.

5

Age at which Rodgers began throwing a football.

Birth Date: December 2, 1983

Birthplace: Chico, California

Height: 6 feet 2 (1.88 m)

Weight: 223 pounds (101 kg)

Team: Green Bay Packers, 2005–

Breakthrough Season: Became the Packers' starting quarterback in 2008

Awards: Super Bowl MVP after 2010 season, 2011 Associated Press Male Athlete of the Year, 2011 NFL MVP

STARTING YOUNG

Rodgers enjoyed football from the start. He would sit and watch entire games when he was just two years old. At the age of five, he started throwing a football. He worked on accuracy by throwing the ball through a tire hanging from a tree in his backyard.

RICHARD SHERMAN DEFENDS WITH CONFIDENCE AND SKILL

San Francisco 49ers quarterback Colin Kaepernick sent a pass to the end zone. It was headed for Michael Crabtree. If Kaepernick and Crabtree connected, the 49ers would head to Super Bowl XLVIII. Richard Sherman made sure they did not. Sherman deflected the pass. Seattle teammate Malcolm Smith intercepted it.

The Seahawks were on their way to the Super Bowl following the 2013 season.

In the Super Bowl, Sherman and the rest of the Seahawks

Sherman led the NFL in interceptions in 2013.

defensive backfield made sure the Denver Broncos never got started. Seattle's defensive backs were known as the "Legion of Boom." They earned the nickname for their hard-hitting style. The Seahawks stopped Denver and quarterback Peyton Manning in a 43–8 victory.

Sherman switched to defense while still in college at Stanford University. He was picked in just the fifth round of the 2011 NFL Draft. He quickly surpassed expectations. Sherman has never been shy about his talent. He boldly talks about his ability in interviews and on social media. His confidence is clear. Sherman challenges opponents. His skills and bold style have disrupted the games of some of the best offensive players in the NFL. Sherman warns other teams against throwing the football his way.

8
Number of passes Sherman intercepted in 2012 and again in 2013.

Birth Date: March 30, 1988

Birthplace: Compton, California

Height: 6 feet 3 (1.91 m)

Weight: 195 pounds (88 kg)

Team: Seattle Seahawks, 2011–

Breakthrough Season: Named All-Pro cornerback in 2012

Awards: All-Pro in 2012 and 2013

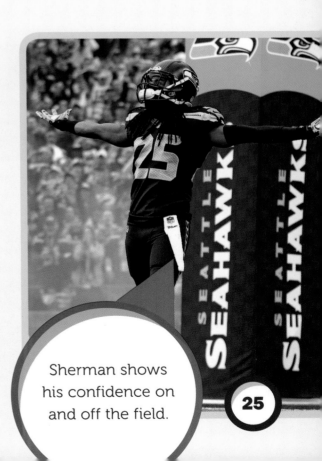

Sherman shows his confidence on and off the field.

J.J. WATT NAMED NFL DEFENSIVE PLAYER OF THE YEAR

Watt rushes in from the outside to sack quarterbacks.

Justin James Watt knows how to disrupt opposing passing games. He is one of NFL's best at sacking quarterbacks. If he can't get to the passer, he leaps and bats down the pass. Either way, the offense has to know where Watt is at all times.

Watt enjoyed hockey as a youngster in Wisconsin. But he stuck to football. Watt won national awards as a defensive end at the University of Wisconsin. The Texans made him the eleventh player picked in the first round of the 2011 NFL Draft. In his second season, Watt was named Associated Press NFL Defensive Player of the Year in 2012. He got all but one of the 50 votes.

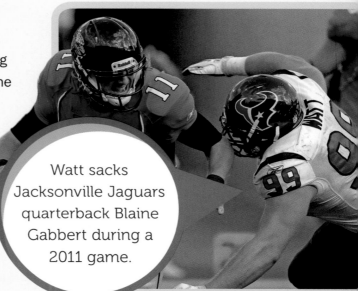

Watt sacks Jacksonville Jaguars quarterback Blaine Gabbert during a 2011 game.

SWITCHING IT UP

Watt started college as a tight end at Central Michigan. But he made a daring move. He switched schools and positions, giving up his scholarship. Watt went to his home state to play defensive end for Wisconsin. His daring move created his path to the NFL.

20.5
Number of sacks Watt recorded in 2012.

Birth Date: March 22, 1989

Birthplace: Waukesha, Wisconsin

Height: 6 feet 6 (1.98 m)

Weight: 290 pounds (132 kg)

Team: Houston Texans, 2011–

Breakthrough Season: Set the team record with 20.5 sacks in the 2012 season

Awards: 2012 NFL Defensive Player of the Year

FACT SHEET

- The National Football League began in 1920. It was originally called the American Professional Football Association. It changed its name in 1922 and began scheduling championship games in 1933. The NFL is made up of 32 teams. These teams are split into the American Football Conference and the National Football Conference. The AFC has many teams from the old American Football League (1960–1969). Most of the NFC is made up of teams that were in the league longer. The conferences have four divisions of four teams each.

- Each spring, NFL teams select players coming out of college during the NFL Draft. Teams take turns picking players. Generally, the teams that had the worst seasons get to pick before those who had success. Sometimes the order changes because teams trade their picks for players or other picks.

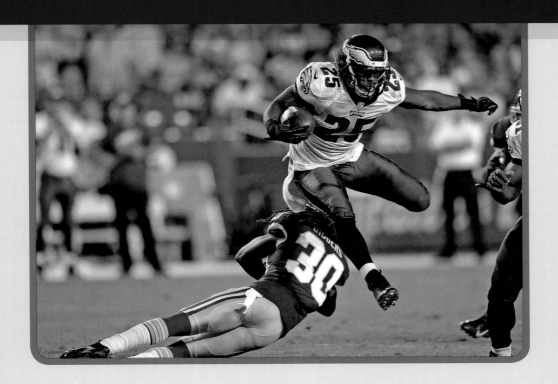

- The first Super Bowl was played in 1967. It was played between the NFL and AFL champions. Most people thought the NFL was the better league. The Green Bay Packers of the NFL won the first two Super Bowls. But in 1969, the AFL's New York Jets pulled off a big upset. They beat the NFL's Baltimore Colts 16–7. That win showed the AFL had some great teams, too. The two leagues merged in 1970. Today, the Super Bowl matches the winners of two conferences—the NFC and AFC.

- The Pro Football Hall of Fame is located in Canton, Ohio. It opened in 1963. It honors the most important people in pro football history. When it opened, 17 players, coaches, and team owners were in its first class. Each year, between four and seven more can be voted in. They are enshrined during a ceremony that happens the first weekend every August. The Hall of Fame includes a museum, a theater, and a research library. Football fans from around the world travel to Canton every year to visit it.

GLOSSARY

contract
A written agreement committing a player to a team. A contract specifies how much the player is paid.

defense
The team trying to stop the other from moving the football down the field and scoring.

NFL Draft
An event held each year in which NFL teams select college football players to join their teams.

offense
The team that has control of the football.

playoffs
Games at the end of the season that decide a champion. When a team loses in the playoffs, its season is over.

Pro Bowl
The NFL all-star game.

receiver
A player who catches passes.

recruited
The process of being sought by colleges to play football.

rookie
A professional football player in his first year.

sack
When a defensive player tackles the offense's quarterback before he can throw a pass.

tackle
Dragging a player to the ground to end a play.

FOR MORE INFORMATION

Books

Garner, Joe, and Bob Costas. *100 Yards of Glory: The Greatest Moments in NFL History*. Boston: Houghton Mifflin Harcourt, 2011.

Sandler, Michael. *Pro Football's Stars of the Defense*. New York: Bearport Publishing, 2011.

Whiting, Jim. *The Story of the Seattle Seahawks*. Mankato, MN: Creative Education, 2014.

Websites

ESPN
www.espn.com

Monday Morning Quarterback
http://www.mmqb.si.com

National Football League
www.nfl.com

Pro Football Reference
www.pro-football-reference.com

INDEX

About the Author

Tom Robinson is the author of more than three dozen books for children. He has written biographies and books about sports, history, and social issues. He lives in Clarks Summit, Pennsylvania.